IT'S ONLY LOVE

RAIN

INDIA • SINGAPORE • MALAYSIA

ISBN
Paperback 979-8-89588-346-4
Hardcase 979-8-89588-961-9

You must keep breaking your heart until it opens

~ Rumi

Poet's Note

Years ago, when I was a demure teen of 15, I was a little girl in her mid-teens when I compiled about seventy out of about a hundred poems I had written into a book and named it 'A Book of Wordless Prayers' I sent the manuscript out to a dozen publishers, all of the publishers that a kid could list in the age of no internet woven deeply into our lives and waited patiently about a month later, I started receiving rejection letters saying that poetry is a dead verse and hence, they cannot take up my book for publishing and if I were to write a book in the future they would be happy to review it.

I was sad for sure but not about to give up from that day on, I started working on my first book I tried my best to work those poems into this book and stay as poetic as possible I was just nineteen when I wrote it But this time I was too busy with life and college to pursue publishing and before I knew it, ten years had passed When I was twenty-seven, I decided to self-publish and the calling and the purpose of my life, my first book: *A Better Man* by Rain, was published And now that I am thirty, it fills me up with courage and joy to see poems everywhere on Instagram Being an old school soul, I want my book of poems out there in the world.

I am full of words I say, don't say, think, don't think, feel, don't feel Writing them down only helps me navigate through life better while staying sane.

So, this is the story of this book The essence, only reading it will help you discover.

Acknowledgement

I am forever grateful to the loves, losses, and moments that inspired these words everything I went through and everyone I met shaped me in their own little ways to make me who I am today As they say, all of the happy moments make you happy, but all of your heartbreaks make you, you Your presence in my life has moulded the rhythms, rhymes, and reflections within these pages.

My family and friends, thank you for your unwavering support, patience, and encouragement Your belief in me has been the sunshine in my darkest of days, and God knows that I have too many of them, that nurtured these poems.

My publisher and my publishing consultant, I appreciate your guidance, expertise, and thoughtful critiques Your input has refined my voice and enhanced the beauty of these verses I thank you for bringing this collection to life Your dedication and professionalism have made this dream a reality.

And to the readers, I offer my deepest gratitude May these poems resonate with your heart, validate your emotions, and inspire you to find solace in the beauty of words.

May you all find love, and when you do, I hope for you to just know for sure that 'It is love'.

Yours,

Rain

Contents

Contents

Contents

See You Again

One of these days, when I'm out in the
streets in the rain

I'll walk past that silly house, hoping to run
into you again

I want to look at you and pass a smile as I used to

And talk about things that don't matter to me or you

Walk with you for a while until we reach that place

Maybe this time, get those flowers for your desk

Ask about the weather, work, and if life is fine

When asked the same, I would look at you and smile

The flowers wilt, and the times change, but the streets
remain

Caring for little but wanting for more,
and always the same

I would ask what brought you back to these streets

Hoping the troubled weather would help you see

That we are doing okay and moving on with ease

This makes hope that you are not back in these streets

If you smile in reply and ask me the reason I'm
walking by

I wish to tell you that I have always had
trouble saying goodbye

And that I come here often, hoping to ease my mind

I know how the question would put you in a bind

The best answer you could give me is your smile

I would know then to take your leave and
give you mine

When we do meet in these streets in the rain someday

I wish you would look at me and come to say, "Hey"

I would want to walk the other way and carry on

The weather might be clear, but my head might not be

*One of these days when I'm in these streets and
run into you*

*I would not know if I should look at you or
even what to do*

I might never walk past the house or go out in the rain

Because these things make me wish I see you again

My Movie

I will turn off the lights tonight, but
I might stay awake

Sit quietly in the dark and flip the pages of my fate

The written words mean more than the words we speak

Of lives that are lived and the promises meant to keep

Nights are too dark and lonesome to read,
but good to feel

Brighter colours and quieter noises, but louder screams

My life plays out like a movie on these unlit walls

A story I must relive until the night breaks into dawn

I don't care much for what I let go of or what I lost

For the losses were too small to outweigh the cost

*I stroll around my house, counting the
things that remain*

The love that I chose to stay makes perfect sense

In the end, life is a simple game that plays itself out

By the end, nothing matters but what we care about

One day, these scenes I remember by heart will fade

This house will crumble, but only the love will stay

Night gets too lonesome, and the movie becomes a bore

Some stories cannot be explained but must be told

So I take out the bottle meant for a special day

I call on you, I pour into two glasses, I sit, and I wait

*I know my story all too well, and I want to
recite it to you*

*For you should know the part you play in
my movie, too*

Just Alright

I hear what all of my friends tell me about you and me

It ruffles me up so badly that not even a drink can fix

They light up a smoke for me as they give me the news

Fearing I might feel that I am easy to replace and use

And I keep convincing them that I am no
longer that fool

I guess they see through me, for I am all
that they can see

I take the news of you as I take a piece of bad memory

Deal with it and put it away so far in my mind
I can't reach

And with time, throw it away so I have space
for better things

*Because some things are far too ugly and
maddening to keep*

*I take a drag and gulp a glass, wondering how
I should feel*

*About the fight I waged to keep the one
I still don't need*

*I admit to going back to the days when you played
me and almost left*

*I am coloured in regret for keeping things that
shouldn't be kept*

*My friends tell me that they pity I played the
fool for so long*

*Pointing out that I should have left when my respect
was wronged*

*They offer smoke and drink, and time to make sure
I am okay*

*I admit it ruffled me up very badly, but I am proud
I didn't break*

After sharing the news, they ask me if I carry any regret

*I tell them no, and you were a lesson that
I won't forget*

As we pour the last drink and light the last cigarette of the night,

I look around the room to count my friends, and I feel just alright

Let It Go

The clock ticks away the day, and then comes
the nightfall

And I will do whatever it takes to keep my
mind off it all

Our story looks so different now that I am no longer
the same

It's easy to see we both changed with the
passing of days

The people we met all those years ago exist
as relics now

I wish we could beat the changing of this
life somehow

If only we could sit and talk like old
friends tonight

*Not recognising me might be the least hurtful thing
this time*

*With each tick of the clock, we are both
wasting away*

*I know you look at me and realise that
tonight is too late*

*I look at you, and I see the mess born
out of my mistakes*

*My mind wanders off to all the things
that no longer exist*

How love changes shape and with it, its entire being'

*This imperfect we love, made and shared,
will always stay*

As a piece of a story we carry in our minds to escape

*The truth that we both deserve a love
that won't change*

*So tonight, when your eyes meet mine,
I want you to see*

*That change is natural, and for a short while,
we were real*

I cannot keep my mind off you tonight
because I know

We did love once, but we've changed, and
it's time to let it go

Colours of Love

With much to say and with the stories that he shares,

He always amazes me with the burden he bears

The strength he carries himself with during despair

*Either adds to itself or claims part of him as
its share's share*

But lately, he has been saying less and thinking more

Wearing less and less of the smile he always wore

In tears, he tells me about that fateful autumn night

When the colours drained and turned black and white

*After words fail him, he shows me a picture
torn in two*

*I was reminded of how she cries that the
world turned blue*

*It's easy to put two halves of the picture together to
make it complete*

*No matter the colour, the picture looks more bitter
than sweet*

It amazes me to see the side of the picture she holds

She tells me she always loses and her cards fold

*Both halves are coloured too differently to
have ever been one*

*I think maybe love is not as simple a game as
easily lost or won*

*Their halves of a picture that they both carry
and show us all*

*Makes me wonder if their grief makes their
love seem small*

*I know the whole story, and I have seen
the whole picture*

*I also know that it's not enough for him to
just miss her*

*The same way he needs more from her
than her tears*

I think maybe they have put behind their best years

*They tell me that when their love was alive,
it coloured everything red*

*But the blues and black & white, who would
want them for themselves?*

Yes

They tell me that we must live our lives before we die

And that death becomes a relief if you lead
a routine life

They ask me if I have found the reason to
keep living on

I give them a smile, thinking of you, and
unknowingly nod

They make me think about how I would escape
the needless pain

And with it, the thoughts of you come
pouring in like rain

I had left my life entirely to chance long before we met

Just passing through life like a piece bound to never fit

The mess I was then is a far cry from what I am now

You are the reason that they keep talking to me about

The reason that we need to escape that tragic fate

Explains why I am standing outside your door again

I know I am half bad, half worse, and a complete mess

Standing in front of you, hoping you would say yes

Act of War

I remember how long we kept fighting an endless war

Till we could not remember what we were fighting for

The deceiving lies and half-truths that you hit me with

Suffocating me with punches until I could not breathe

In the pauses that I could not do without

You kept killing me with your unfounded doubts

I hope bruising my heart has brought you some peace

Knowing I am out of love should cure your disease

The blame that you put on me is just an excuse

To this cruel, one-sided game, we have been reduced

You come and go and come again as you please

Seeing me as an option rather than a promise to keep

*It has been years, and I can still recall every
time I was hit*

*I am over this thing I cannot call love and
want to quit*

I will move on and heal, but you will stay the same

Treating people like an act of war or a ruined game

If I do not give up and close all my windows and doors

*Someone will love me right, and my faith will
be restored*

When I forget the lies, the punches, the game, and you

*Then bruises will heal, and soon my heart will beat
like new*

*I wish to feel that I am more than a ruined game or an
act of war*

*Someone who can fight for love and for love is worth
fighting for*

Damn Your Love

We walk the same road tonight as all those years before

I am wearing a different heart than the one
I always wore

I wish it felt better to see you after these years
than it does

You take me back to when this wretchedness
was called love

With tears and shame, you ask me to change my mind

But now that I can see, how do I go back
to being blind?

The disrespect and the curses lie bare between
you and me

There's a ring on your finger, but you are
here begging me

*Does he know you're doing all this to turn
two into three?*

*I would never want any of your broken love again,
but does he?*

*The innate desire for improvement always comes at
the cost of losing everything*

*I guess some things look better when gone,
just out of reach*

*I see you for who you are without tainting
my vision with dreams*

Now that my heart is stronger, I wear it on my sleeves

*I wonder why you have come back to walk
with me tonight*

*You know, talking about how it had been will not
make it right*

*I hope the tears you are filled with clear
your greedy sight*

*The shame should grow until it is big enough to
swallow you*

*To remind you of the reason you are left with nothing
to gain or lose*

*I hope it hurts you to know that you are
the reason I walked away*

*My heart is too different now to ever settle for
the abuse again*

*You cry as you yell that you want whatever we had
between us*

*I look at you and think, if this is how you love, then
damn your love*

This Love

The story goes that when a heart madly in love breaks,

It starts to believe that love is dead, or a plain mistake

There is only so much love that an aching
heart can hold

As it keeps bleeding out until the love finally grows cold

I was the one to fight for love until it left me
cold with regret

My sorrow had become a part of me long
before we met

Everything I built had begun to decay before
you walked in

You showed me beauty in the ruins that I hide
beneath my skin

*I have had love before, but not as strong as I have it
with you*

*Love can be different things and still be real, as long as
it is true*

*Just a kiss, a touch, a laugh, a smile, or even just a
simple look*

*Puts my mind at ease, and for a while, everything
looks good*

*I stand here in front of you, hearing your stories
with a smile*

*When I am with you, I do not ever want
anything but more time*

*You listening to my stories assures me that this is our
safe place*

*The one place we all look for when we
just need to escape*

*I know I cannot put any of it into words,
but it is easy to see*

*You have been changing me for the better,
and with it, my belief*

I believed that my heart had bled out and that love was dead

But right here and now, I have started to believe in you instead

I know that love is ever-growing and never the same for any of us

Just know, no matter what comes and goes, I will die for this love

I Miss You

I listen for your footsteps all the time around this house

*Accepting that everything is better when
you are around*

*A deafening silence falls upon this house
every time you go*

*My mind begins its torture, and the time
seems to go by slow*

*It begins by replaying the seasons this
house has withstood*

*The rain falls as cold as ice, pouring harder
than it should*

*I remember the unforgiving winter as if
it has never left*

The snow might be beautiful, but the
chill soon begins its effect

The fall that waits for summer as it watches
the leaves shake

Leaving only after the trees have become bare
in its wake

The kind summer that the whole house
waits for follows you

With your footsteps, the leaves grow and
the trees look new

The day and the night take their turns as
they always do

But the summer stays with its sun as long as
I have you

The house feels like a ruin without the echo
of your steps

You weaken and wear off the effect the chilly
winter left

I hope you come with the summer without
having to go

Sometimes realising takes time to realise
what you already know

I've never needed anyone like I have begun
to need you

The absence of your footsteps makes me realise
I miss you

Everything Else

I usually drive around aimlessly in my car by
myself at night

Counting all the chances I had to do everything right

Sometimes I take the same turns and repent
all night long

Coming up with ways, I wish I could trade
all of my wrongs

There are some nights when happy thoughts
cloud my head

But I cannot help thinking they might be
awfully misread

The darkness of the night is quiet and has a
beauty to it

That leads to a hope that nothing is too
broken to be fixed

I drive alone, hoping that I might find a way
to love myself

For the scarred ones, don't accept love but
rather defend

The thought of the might-have-been don't let me sleep

I accept that some things we lose, while others we keep

As I take the same turn again tonight for the
hundredth time,

I recall the times when I crossed the place where I had
drawn the line

Some turns just make me see the scars that
I try to hide

They colour me like paint that I can neither
remove nor dye

The night makes me see the beauty that
I love so much

Planting a fear that I will taint everything
with my touch

This endless cycle goes on repeat until the
break of dawn

The line between the loved and the
unloved is redrawn

Each night, I keep going through the same
cycle of repent

It's funny how I can curse myself and
still love everything else

A Ghost

I lock the front door and turn out the
lights again tonight

Following a ritual that weighs out a part of
me every time

The darkness silently creeps in and makes it
easier to see

Who I am and who I've always been after
everyone leaves

I light a cigarette or two to make it easier to
look at myself

How many I will need to light tonight is
anybody's guess

My thoughts give in and follow the trails of the smoke

Letting the smoke take me wherever it wants me to go

It takes me to the window, and I stare out like a ghost

*Everything I have ever loved and lost rises
up with smoke*

*The things I never wished for linger as smoke
in the room*

Their foul smell makes the smoke smell like perfume

*The smoke shows me why I hide behind
smoke every night*

*For what I see in the smoke always earns
my own, despite*

*I need another cigarette to love who
I am after everyone leaves*

*A ghost that is enveloped in smoke,
which no one really sees*

This Shadow

—◆◆—

I watch this shadow play and disappear
into these dreams

The doors are always unlocked, but it never
seems to leave

Its' footsteps don't make any sound, but I always know

Where this shadow hides and where it wants me to go

A temper lost, a lesson learnt, and
the shadow that came

Unlike the tears in rain, they do not hide
my wicked shame

These richly coloured dreams of mine are
fading to grey

Losing their colours every time the
shadow comes to play

Maybe the shadow is an empty space
that replaced you

Or the form my regrets took before they lost
the colour blue

The shadow follows my dreams and asks
if you left or if I let go

It keeps coming back to ask me something
none of us know

After I come to terms with this shadow that
refuses to leave,

I will dream again and in colours
that shadows can't bleed

Till then, I will watch this shadow play
with colours and steal

Hoping to ask, what is the reason the colours
and you decided to leave?

Two Stories of Love

Some say love and heartache are both one and the same

For them, everything is set to play out like
an unfair game

They look out of their window, and all
they see is a barren tree

And logically sell love as an undying
hunger and endless need

They think the sky is always cloudy and grey,
and when it rains

The bare tree gets wet, but all they notice
are unwashed stains

For some, life and love are two sides of a
journey they are on

Every badly written part of theirs only ushers in a
breaking dawn

The garden that overlooks their window is never
barren or bare

Because they know that there is always room
for new leaves

Looking at the same tree under the same sky
makes me wonder

The magic that makes the difference in the
things that are and were

I know I see both the barrenness and the
new leaves of the tree

It renders me helpless not knowing which
story to put my belief in

Love can be beautiful and kind, but also
unforgiving and unjust

Like the tree under the coloured sky and
everything that makes us

I count the new leaves, but it is so hard to
wipe off all the dust

The thoughts of love come, and with them come
thoughts of you and I

People may say differently, but the lost love
makes all of them cry

I see the colours of the sky and the green
leaves coming through

And I know that the only love I will ever
believe in is you

My Weight

They tell me that everything is okay and that
I'm out of line

But should I be blamed for not knowing
how to be fine?

Some have it worse than me, while some have
it the same

They don't get the reason why I just can't give
in to my fate

Existence seems like an unguarded prison
I cannot flee

As the days and nights go on in an endless
cycle on repeat

The weight of my being gets very heavy and
turns to guilt

*I know I will turn into a mess, no matter
how I am rebuilt*

*It's not good to be so hard on myself,
but I cannot stop*

*Hoping one day I'll learn how to be fine
when I am not*

*They act as if I need a reason for feeling
what I feel*

*Like feelings vanish if there's no reason for
their being*

*I am broken, and I am remade time and
time again*

Like a curse, it keeps putting me back in my place

*A moment of grief, and I come undone like
a house of cards*

*For every place I break or crack, I am
left with scars*

*I look for the escape throughout the days
and nights*

*The strength it takes to brave it all drains
me of life*

I feel sad and lost every time I know
I am about to break

And the tears that I cry keep on adding to
my weight

Once More

I have been through it all, and I have heard
it all before

And you are telling me the same old story once more

I have lived through this story, and I know how it ends

It always ends with a broken heart that's hard to mend

This story is sweet to listen to and live but hard to
get over

I remember the sound of breaking as the end gets closer

My heart was broken once, and I remember
it all so well

This story is cursed to betray the one who listens or tells

I feel the difference when you tell me this story
with a smile

I want to listen to you call it love for longer
than a while

You make me wonder how the story will go this time

Teaching me that it's time to let the heartbreak slide

The curved smile that you wear as you take my hand,

Tells me that you know it all well, and you understand

A story, a heartbreak, a love, and then there's you

I didn't know I had the strength to make it through

I have mended my broken heart on my own before

And this story you tell shouldn't interest me anymore

But your smile makes me want to listen once more

New Day

If I count the endless nights that I have spent this way,

Would it excuse the new bottle I have opened today?

I wonder if these empty bottles add a sadder detail

And be written off as another messed-up fairy tale?

A bunch of small wins held up by a larger mistake

That comes undone with some whisky and ginger ale

I look at the bottle that's never full and pour from it

Knowing well that my sorrows may drown,
but still live

Half of my life is stored in this glass and
half in my head

A series of mistakes until the alcohol takes me for dead

But tonight, I am alive, and so I drink to all those times

I believed that everything was meant to be by design

A life of chasing wild dreams, committing horrid sins

Knowing well when my story will begin and end

The night changes, and I am counting glasses of wine

A ritual of drinking that ends before I begin, being fine

The story I've lived is more of a tragedy than a fairytale

The growing number of empty bottles is another sad detail

Tonight is the night to drown sorrows and wither away

If I survive tonight, then tomorrow will be a brand new day

The Door

They neither know nor understand what love is about

The derision of everything I feel fills me with doubt

I carry the weight of my being wrapped up in my head

Are there words that I have not yet written or said?

_A thousand times I have walked up to your
unopened door_

_To lay my heart open and tell you what you
already know_

The shadows that I see from outside nudge me to leave

They have seen my heart break and still worn on sleeves

_It's no surprise that I see their concern for
me as a threat_

I know it's an unwanted love, but I don't
want you to forget

At times, I think they do know better about
love and loss

They tell me it's good to hold out, but better
to move on

The shadows, the unopened door, and this
love of mine

They break my broken heart as a punishment
for this crime

I knock on your door again to say it all like
a chore I must complete

But this unopened door and this love are what
a loss truly is

The doubt they planted grows like a weed
I cannot pull out

Covering this love entirely and teaching me
to live without

It weighs up what I am losing or what I never
won to claim

*Their derision never moved me, but I have
nothing to my name*

*Shadows behind the door remind me of what
was not mine to keep*

*And I know one day what you lost tonight
won't let you sleep*

Come Again

I hold my breath while seasons peak and then change

The sun ushers in the changes, but it remains the same

Rain or shine, these miles that separate have withstood

But with time, everything fades away,
just like it should

A picture from the winter is burnt in the back
of my mind

Another bleak night of gloom, but we had
found the light

The light will burn, and I can see more
clearly than before

When the storm gathers, as a beacon,
it guides me ashore

We spent the summer passing through
the roads of this town

Learning to let go of the heartaches
without breaking down

As the days changed, the summer passed in
the blink of an eye

Though I deal with the distance fine,
my heart still sinks

I wait for you as I see the leaves that have
begun to fall

The light still burns, and suddenly no distance
seems small

But now, after the seasons have come and
gone like they do

I look back at those times, and I hope you know
I just miss you

The sun changes the days, but the light
remains the same

I look at these miles as I wait for winter
to come again

Read It Again

I pick up my pen to vent these feelings,
time and time again

Writing every little thing down on these pages,
but it's all in vain

For what I write does not add up and just
confuses the most

Your two sides are like the desert sun and
the lingering ghost

The sun may light up the days, but it still
cruelly burns my skin

Like a mirage on a summer day, it is full
of nothing but deceit

The heart plays along with the game that
you play so well

Pretending not to hear the horrors that
the ghost has to tell

But my ears stay full as my skin continues to
burn in the sun

My broken heart juggles the love between
the lost and the won

The ghost of the love you broke haunts me
time and time again

I may write it all down in a beautiful rhyme,
but pain is still pain

My burnt skin makes me look like the
ghost that haunts me

A pile of hurtful memories that took
this form so I may see

It's common to avoid the sun when the
skin begins to burn

And hurtful memories all leave when dealt
with, not to return

This love game that you play has kept me
blind for so long

Closed my eyes to the mirage and the ghost,
just to play along

I'm so worn down that I cannot continue
like we have just begun

The ghost and the game have broken me,
and now I avoid the sun

I have tried to write it all down, but this
pain is so hard to explain

So, if this poem that I wrote confuses you,
please read it again

Lie to Me

The night-time falls, and it clears the pictures
in my head

And how they mess me up all night is
anybody's guess

I know your deceitful lies that you use to get
your way

Without them, I admit, you and I could
have been okay

You turn everything into a war that I could
never win

Your lies are the loaded gun that never
misses its hit

The trick that you always play to get your
way with me

Though I admit, it fooled me till now, but now
it has worn thin

Now I look at you for what you have always
been inside

This will impale your conceited self, but
I know it won't die

I pity whoever you will pick to play with after
I am gone

The night will untangle my knotted heart
before the dawn

Your lies and your deceit clear the
picture of disbelief

I am letting go of you like a tree shedding
dead leaves

Some things become a fond memory though
lost to time

While some stay and treat you like an
unforgivable crime

But you are among those who will be gone
and forgotten

*Like the times you pick yourself up after
you've fallen*

*I will be at peace even if you or none of
this remains*

*Therefore, don't look into my eyes and lie
to me again*

Your Name

I watch the passing of the seasons as the days change

*The sun warms me again, and the snowflake
falls again*

*Now, this home of mine has begun to feel so
very strange*

*As I slowly lose my mind while counting
the passing days,*

They tell me to share whatever bothers me as of late

*But it's hard to find words and harder to
take your name*

So it's easier to stay home and count the days as I wait

*I pray you come for me before death calls me to the
grave*

A picture of them trying to pull me away
always stays fresh

My choice to fight them to love alone spares
me no friend

The countless days and the changing seasons
welcome me

And teach me it's ok to take your name but to
have no belief

Summer moves on, and the days begin to slip
into the night

But the long nights don't sleep at all once
the winter arrives

I lose, little by little, every time I take your
name as it is meant

My home collects the remains of my mind
and still asks for rent

You will hear the story and the counting
I have done in your name

As I kept waiting for you, losing friends,
home, and my sanity

*Everyone knows how I fought and waited as the
seasons changed*

*To take your name with ease is still worth
everything in the end*

*They will take the heart out of me, and the
days just like to play*

*I wait, and I know I will greet death with
the uttering of your name*

The Blame

I am the fickle blame that keeps shifting with such ease

That always comes and goes like a cold autumn breeze

Like the downpour that eases yet agitates your mind

Leaves you soaked with the doubt that turns you blind

I become the soft snow that engulfs everything in white

A little like your voice that always wants
you to be right

When the sunlight shines, all is bright
enough to be seen

Nothing remains to hold but us, with
everything in between

But the blame that moves so easily between you and me

Turns just the two of us into an ever so crowd of three

This game of fickle blame that we play, we play to win

*The prize is the losing of love, but we wear
it on our skin*

This routine that we hold onto like an irrefutable belief

Has reduced me to the blame you keep putting on me

So, now I am the autumn breeze that comes and goes

Like it should, before any new blame can be put on me

*Going separate ways will break our hearts once
and for all*

*But it is better than staying together and
still drifting apart*

*I am the hope for you to remember us for
all we had become*

*And not just the game we kept playing that
was never won*

With You

That night, I was alone with all I had become
and my disbelief

I heard you're coming like a song, and a
year has passed since

You came in like the tide no one expects,
nor prepares for

But everyone welcomes the relief from
the bloody war

I was the island where no ships dared to
seek harbour

Rough on the surface, but the skin still cut
like the skin

I know the more they knew of me, the
less they understood

*Like the burning of a witch, they see and
then forget for good*

*They called me evil and coloured me black
with shame*

*Little did they know that with enough water,
all colours fade*

*Thought I had lost and been hurt with nothing
left to dream*

*Yet, with your hello, you kept changing the
way things seem*

*Now, this longing that takes hold of me
always wins*

*I am a never-breaking rock, but like a reed,
I bend to your winds*

*You calm the voices in my head and put my
mind at ease*

*Night after night, I win against the demons
that fight me*

*I look at you, your smile, and I am home
wherever I stand*

For my whole life, I will be where your waters
meet my land

How I was before you is anybody's guess, yet
no one has a clue

So, tell me, what is a lifetime compared to
this year with you?

Your Ship

I fail to assure all of my friends that I am
as good as any

They get worried sick wherever I have had
one too many

And my mind plays its tricks on me, and
like a child, I yield

Then these feelings surface instead of
staying concealed

They see the redness in my eyes and stains on
my cheek

I am petrified of being seen and of the help
I should seek

The kind look they give me before they ask
about you and I

Breaks my heart, for they know we are good
but not fine

And the smile I reply with feels no less than a sin

It will tell you that you are a prize worth
scheming to win

But I am the rose people leave on their
beloved's grave

Thrown after they wilt, else no one touches
but the dead

They tell me you will give up when the times
get uncertain

Like a drug that had promise but just failed to
be the cure

They counsel as if they know love is ugly and
never enough

That we die of bleeding out too much rather
than the cut

If they knew love like we do, then maybe
they'd know the touch

Drives away the doubts for which drinks will
never be enough

*They shy away from love as if they have loved
and let it slip*

*I am mad enough to love deeper and to
drown with your ship*

Remade

Everything has remained fresh in my mind to this day

It's funny how I wanted death in the name of fate

And you'd find it sadder that I had planned how I'd go

Life tested me, and like a sandcastle, I crumbled so

I might be easy to see, but you saw the dirty secret I hid

Your helping hand was like the life begging to be lived

I was the festering ruins that fell more than it stood

Nature was taking its course, eating me up for good

Little did I know that the broken could be remade

You helped me be remade and rediscover my trade

I'm keeping the smile that you gave me like an oath

*To embrace life in all its forms and have room
for growth*

*I know now that nothing is ever as bad as in
our heads*

*Times change, and hope is to life what beads
are to thread*

*We all have our demons that we win against
or lose to*

*Learning not to give up is everything that
gets us through*

*I hope you see me looking at you as you
look at me tonight*

You are all the reason that I found a reason to not die

*Now I know that it's fair of life to break me
time and again*

*But because of you, I am stronger, and I will
always be remade*

Broken Goodbye

*Years and years have passed, but we are still
in this war*

*The warmth has faded, and the good deeds
written off*

*I wish for us to be reminded of that magic
and that love*

But not of the problem thereof

*We know by now that this time one is
better than two*

A fire that burnt red is now turning black and blue

*The game of sorry's and punches has
grown old and stale*

*Some trains take you home, but some just
stay derailed*

I accept the truth of it all, and I know
I have to let go of you

It's hard to see that we started to move on
but never knew

I am not sure what to call it, but I know
I cannot call it love

We might hope for it to matter, but in the
long run, it doesn't

They tell me that when it feels like home,
you know it's true

This field of battle is exactly what has
fallen through

I have no regrets nor pride in whatever
became of you and me

No tears for the pain, but only for the part
of me that died

Time heals every wound, and I will leave too,
as you left

For I have love left in me enough to not
remain bereft

But here and now, I stand with you,
holding a broken heart

Knowing endings hurt, but they pave the
way for a new start

So, as we prepare to quit this war and
say our goodbyes,

Promise me you won't forget me and the
tears in our eyes

This Roof

The beautiful and the ugly, I have seen all sides of you

I love and want all of you, and I will walk
right through

You have seen my good and my worst, highs and lows

We stand strong when we are far, just as we do close

This beautiful feeling is all I feel as I raise a toast

Drunk on wine and love, I see their looks, but I ignore

My friends disapprove, like they know all
about me and you

Given the high stakes, the judgement will
never be good

I hear and see it all as they open another
bottle of red

*All of the stares make me want to love you
more instead*

We evade their mocking comments and empty stares

Like a poison so potent that it taints the vase

They tell me that I should test the water before I dive

Because sometimes you lose everything in the tide

There will always be a reason for me to pull away

Life and troubles always have got in love's way

*Right now, my ears belong to them, but my
heart is yours*

For your love, all I have is room and no walls or doors

So, I hope you do what I do when I hear these things

Trust my drunken heart and wear my hand as a ring

My heart cannot be persuaded, moved or changed

For the love you make me feel is the roof over my head

Misused

I've been hearing the same routine from
everyone lately

The voices change, but the idea of love remains
the same

They have a certain path to it that they are
happy to tread

Thinking they can mould me with the words
they have said

Love had me on my knees with my hands
open towards the sky

It was more of a blessing and less of a pain to
be left out to dry

I know I am fairly hard to get over but much
easier to leave

The belief is so inside my bones that I cannot cleave

*Wounded and broken by their hateful words
that cut like knives*

*Love is a bloody war where no one dies; still,
only the dead survive*

*Years and years have passed, and the times
continue changing*

*I have learnt that life is a game and to win,
I must keep rearranging*

*There's no reason left to believe again and
let love play its' part*

*I have thought of all the ways you can and
will break my heart*

*When the time comes to move on and
be okay without you*

*They will tell me to begin again and to
look for something new*

*That's a wonder how they rebuild themselves
with such ease*

*For me, the longing kills much faster than
any disease*

*After hearing everything they have to tell
me about love,*

*My mind is still the same, but my heart
keeps waiting for more*

*The love I have for you is much stronger,
but I'm bound to lose*

*Everyone knows choosing me is a choice
that remains misused*

Cost of Love

*I have always been taught that everything
we do is a trade*

*To exercise caution when in love's corner
of the marketplace*

It is easiest to be fooled by a deceitfully beautiful heart

*They warned that half-truths and full lies are
one of their arts*

*Luck smiles on some, and they do find a lost
gem to treasure*

*Keeping it from being lost is a harder task by
a huge measure*

*For the cost of love more often outweighs
the cost of loss*

And rarely helps to say a little prayer and
let hope get it across

The heart in me was bruised, healed,
and beating strong

I was not looking for love and not wanting
a place to belong

But the pulling I still feel is almost oh
so impossible to resist

The fool that I have become will trade
my life away to be kissed

Heartbreaks remind me of the caution
I must take in this trade

You know it took courage for me to lay all
of my cards bare

And when you look at me as though
I am all that you can see,

Like you see the beauty and the truth that
will ever come to be

For the sake of the deal we have made,
we are putting all at stake

*I only ask for love when the time comes for
the broken to break*

*My life to keep and to call your own will be
enough to get by*

*To be fine with the little things is the art
I have learnt not to die*

*So, the cost of love that we have paid seems
like a fair trade*

*I know now that magic does find you in
the strangest of ways*

Gone

You will keep finding me in little things
when I'm gone

Like in this letter and the curves of the
words I've drawn

So, read it and keep it close to you to
remember me by

Believe that death can't take everything, sometimes

They cannot bury me with my body for now,
I am you

I will follow you wherever you go and
whatever you do

Nights will come, and you will see the stars
shine down

When you miss me, know in the soft light
I'll be found

I will be the roses you keep in the corner of your room

And the wind that will blow when you wear perfume

The days when you just don't want to get up
from bed

I hope you will read this letter and find
strength instead

For all the times when it will rain a bit too
hard on you,

Remember, the sun always finds a way to
shine through

And when the time comes, asking you to let go again

Just go and get a new red rose to keep on your desk

Save this letter for times when you cannot find
your strength

Read it and keep re-reading it until you find
me again

Keep me close to you in the pocket of your best dress

Carry me with my words with you through every mess

*Though we may one day belong to worlds that
break in two*

*Every time you smile and miss me, I will
come back to you*

*Remember, I am a part of you and the letters
I've drawn*

*This letter in your hand may remind you that
I'm never gone*

Flowers On My Grave

I have died cold several and many times before

Also been buried alive with all of my love just
for show

How many more deaths and live funerals can
I endure?

It depends on my abating heart that does not
love anymore

They told me love is too heavy to be kept on your chest

I found hard proof when I was given no
liberty to express

All of this love is mine to keep, or so they
keep telling me

But the trouble is that this love will be the
death of me

*You say it is a poison that colours your damned
heart blue.*

*This heart has worn down thin with this love
you don't want*

*Your haunting words have become the flowers
on my grave*

*And the love you never gave me flows like poison
in my veins*

*Now looking back at how death took my
heart and my love*

*It feels just unsettlingly wrong, like a train
leaving from home*

*Regardless of love that didn't live and tears
that overflowed*

*There's no denying that ours was a story
meant to be let go*

*So, having to attend another funeral for me
isn't very sad*

*I will still cry for this love of mine that I lost,
more than I had*

*I had died many times before, but my end
comes from you*

*For the poison that flows in me turns me so
darn painfully blue*

*The flowers on my grave will forever be
put up for show*

*To shout to the world that this heart does
not love anymore*

My Pain

They told me to drown my pain in my tears
like it's a joke

I was convinced that the answer is a bottle or a smoke

They told me to pack my sorrows up like old clothes

Leave it somewhere where my mind neither
comes nor goes

But they failed to see that now, sadness is in my bones

My heart, my life, my love, and all of me now it owns

The dreams and fears of mine are all too real to me

But they say they don't believe in what they cannot see

I tried being drunk on my tears day in and night out

Even poured a glass of red to leave no room for doubt

But my demons, they keep coming back to me
like a curse

They shadow even my happy moments,
making them worse

I rise with moons, sleep with the suns, and
cry with skies

Living like this is wearing me down, and
not a soul realises

A question lies at the bottom of the red that
I pour every day

If it is so easy to die, then why is it so hard to
be on my way?

They tried to convince me life is a gift we
don't throw away

But it disappeared just as easily as the
smoke of a cigarette flame

They can tell me to drown my pain in my tears
like it's a joke

But nothing makes sense to me like my pain,
red, and smoke

The Mask

The men are masquerading as the men they
wish they were

And the women looking prettier without
knowing what for

I stand in the corner with my mask on,
sipping champagne

Pretending not to see them at a party the
plan for which I never made

It is hard to meet someone who is what
they seem to be

As I hide behind my mask, playing the night
out like a sad movie

I hide myself like an ugly secret, fearing who
I have become

The love that I carry becomes a knife so sharp
that it will cut

So I maintain my distance as if I am doing
everyone a favour

Acting like a damsel in distress, waiting for a
prince to save her

But feeling like the witch that needs to be burnt
at the stake

And thinking that living our lives like this
party is a huge mistake

The mask gets harder to hold onto as I keep
drinking champagne

Everyone will say yes to, "Am I not the ugliest
villain ever to be made?"

The men keep masquerading for the women
they like, to be liked

And the women keep getting prettier, playing
hard to come by

My champagne gets me drunk, and I forget the
need to hide

*When the mask falls off, I will be the only real
one in this life*

*And I only hope for you to see me for what
I am, was, and will be*

*That I am to be kept like a promise and not
hidden away in secrecy*

My Love

I will go up in flames one day with all the love
I have guarded

The fire will melt memories of the souls that
left me hardened

People come and go like the wind on a
summer's day

That turns to cold snow with the winter;
it's just the life's way

The secret of love is to learn to let them come
and let them go

To keep their love in memories and to hold and
cherish them so

The grief of loss also stays, and I have learnt to
guard it with life

Life has shown me to love like a madman
and guard like a knight

I have met and loved many before, and I
will meet people again

But the love I cannot lose again stands in the
way of my defence

The warmth of the light that engulfs you tonight
is like a dream

Makes the way of it all seem to me like a
well-laid-out scheme

The light I see has cleared up the fog, and
I can finally see

What life is, instead of guarding the loss,
I need to set it free

Love comes and love leaves; it is the way
it has always been

Summer's day breeze or winter's snow reflects
what's within

*I will be warm and bright with light when
it is my time to be lit up*

*The memories will ignite the fire to warm
and enshrine my love*

The Normal Way

*I have learnt to hold onto my breath as if
I am drowning*

*Watch you leave as the beat in my chest kept
pounding*

*I will learn to let go of you as I have learnt to
love you*

*The new ways of life will burn like an
absolute truth*

*I will be obedient as a yew to tender all days
of my youth*

*But when I am old and grey with nothing to
lose but life,*

*I will come to you, knock on your door,
asking for your time*

When you open the door and see me there,
ailing and frail

Will there be hope and a chance for us to fall
in love again?

I have left you to your life at your will, when
I have my youth

Waiting for the time when it will be my
chance to call on you

May the life you choose to live have everything,
and more

I will listen to all your stories when I come to
your door

The life you chose for me might just end up
drowning me

Whatever happens, just know I will do my
best to breathe

For I have learnt to breathe even while
I am drowning

Replaying your leaving as my heart has
stopped counting

I hope you wait for the time when we are
both old and grey

Maybe then, I will have a chance to breathe
the normal way

Town to Town
Depth of Soul

I wonder why you drive all the time, going from
town to town

Do you think anyone will miss having you around?

Or maybe you missed something that you
have left behind

Maybe you need a life to live that is not lived by design

I feel you will stay when you find the thing you look for

Or something that quiets the loudness of the inside war

You have gathered no moss, like an ever-rolling stone

This freedom comes with a cost of having no
one to own

With each drive in the depths of your soul,
a journey begins

With every step, embracing the unknown and
your own skin

When you gaze into the mirror, do you see
a stranger's eyes?

Your laughter, your tears, your triumphs and
your strife

This journey of yours unwinds with the
gentle flow of this life

Leading you home as you embrace the beauty
of what you hide

I think I know why you drive all the time,
going from town to town

You are looking for yourself where you don't
need to feel torn

Hot Summer's Day

This is a story about the clear haze of a hot
summer's day

When we found ourselves looking for love in
each other's way,

The love felt like a flame burning bright,
like a fire anew

Melting away all our fears and giving way to
this love for two

Your eyes, a window; your skin, a canvas full
of all colours of love

For a moment, the light of the flame burnt
brighter than the sun

A silent whisper broke the silence with a
promise and a choice

Our hearts found rest in the silence as if it had
heard a voice

Your touch ignited the flame like the bonfire on
a winter's night

I found a home in your embrace, and
my darkness found light

Memories of the day still linger like perfume in
the air of my room

Showing all the ways my heart is mended and
now belongs to you

Through the light of the burning flame of this love,
I find my way

With every breath I'll take, I promise I'll love true,
come what may

The story of clear haze and love that started on a
hot summer's day

When we found love burning in the embrace
in the light of the flame

The courage I have found to keep this love that
is made for two

And this mended heart that reminds that
now it belongs to you

It's Only Love

One aching truth I was told was it's only
love till it's not

Time will take away every love you have ever caught

With all your thoughts, a restless mind puts up its fight

Correcting a wrong that doesn't want to be set right

The guilt wraps around your body with
a suffocating hold

But this story of mine and yours, is it not very,
oh, so old?

There is only one way this story has ever ended
on my side

I had it all to gain, something to lose,
that's almost mine

The grey that we live in is blacker than we
see it to be

For it is a truth that it is love when it's two
and not three

The suffocating hold lets me breathe as I
accept my loss

It is only love until it was not It was only
love until it was not

With all your thoughts, a breaking mind
lost the fight

I put at stake something that was not even mine

One truth I learnt by trying was that it's
only love until it's not

Time took away every love I had never truly caught

It is only love until it is not, it was only
love until it was not

Life after You

*Your absence and your memories echo through
my days*

*Like a dear old friend, it keeps crossing all the
paths I take*

*The swallowing void that you left, that time
failed to erase*

*The world moves on with its life, and yet, here with
you, I remain*

*Frozen in and cursed to haunt like a ghost for life,
my little lane*

*I look around these paths I take, only to find
an empty space*

A void that stares at me like an old enemy from
a lonely place

No dawn breaks in my path; no new day begins
in my way

A memory of love and a heart that beats,
yet still does not live

I see that love is never the same, always grieves
but still forgives

My heart is shattered by your parting, and my
soul is so worn

My world crumbled, my path became lonely,
and my future was torn

I search for the love you gave me, like I know
I will find it again

The absence and the memories refuse to let go
of me in that way

For every breath, every heartbeat, it's hard to
believe it too

That I was so blind to it when I had the chance
not to lose you

My road, my life, is lonely, but it is full of memories of me and you

I will stay here, haunting like a ghost, because there's no life after you

It is Love

I have learnt a lot in my life that has proven enough

With the ups and downs of life, it has taught me much

Yet, in your eyes, all that I know and learnt fade
to dust

I catch a glimpse of tomorrow, feeling that
knows no rust

Every truth I upheld, every certainty that I
knew for sure,

Fades from view beneath the weight of your love,
like a cure

In your gaze, I find the only love that is ever meant
to stay

A love that is oh so true that it makes everything
else vain

All I thought I had learnt in life, all I thought
I had found

Drowns out the noise in my head without
making a sound

As dawn breaks, the shadows, a love lives,
and a hope revives

In every moment with you, my mended heart
learns to thrive

All worries are left behind, like dead and
fallen autumn leaves

As the story of our love unfolds, holding onto one belief

All the things I know and learn just fail to be enough

I look into your eyes and I know for certain
that it is love

I'm Yours

These stolen moments are all we share

Goodbye kisses and longing with despair

Joyful hellos come with a warm embrace

That brings chances to make and celebrate

Things to remember you by when you're away

They grow in number with each passing day

Nights seem empty, and days are too long

This distance seems so unforgiving and wrong

It has been a while since the last time we met

I wonder if you know how easy everything gets

Loving is so hard, and yet, harder is the wait

But if it is for you, no trouble seems too great

Days come to rest, and nights pass away

Little by little, love grows and takes its shape

The days may seem long, but time always flies

The way you run to me assures me you are mine

Stolen moments, this love, and so much more

The things that make us may remind you I'm yours

Dear Diary

Dear diary, let us both pray that I don't fall
in love again

I think we both just know that I can't go through
that pain

We both get so worried when I write about him
so often

How a smile greets me when I see him, and
our gazes soften

I have known love before, but it feels like a
different life

With the thought comes all the pain with which
love is rife

But even as I write, I feel the fuzzy feelings peaking
deep within

A fragile hope and a stronger pull, where a new love might begin

Though fear grips me, I can't unsee the light I see when I see him

There are moments when everything fades; it's just him and me

I promise you that I beg to stop, but my heart won't always listen

But a life without this fuzzy feeling cages my heart like a prison

Yet still, I pray for caution, for something to break my imminent fall

For I've been taught that love, though beautiful, demands it all

So diary, stay with me, hold my hand through thick and thin

And pray that if I love again, it won't leave scars on my skin

Heartache, pain, doubt, and all the things with that love runs rife

*Feels like an ache in my heart, twisting, hurting,
like a knife*

*So, though it's true that I cannot handle another
heartbreak,*

*Please pray, if I fall in love again, it is here to stay
Yours, Rain*

This Game

I tried my best to be cautious, to play this game safe

*Yet, in the end, I was left abandoned like
an unwanted waif*

Diary, just know I never meant to cause harm or hurt

*Maybe this game is for the smart,
cunning, and alert*

As I write to you, I feel ashamed of being such a fool

Forever thinking that I can win this game for two

*I thought, perhaps, if I stayed kind and
loving and true*

That this dance would finally be one meant for two

*But it seems that the cards were stacked
from the start*

And in this cruel game, in my blindness,
I wagered my heart

Now I sit with the deafening silence that
muffles my ache

I begin to wonder what parts of me I had to forsake

Yet even in this loss, I have found my strength
to stand

To gather the pieces from the waif with my
trembling hand

Perhaps the game we played was never mine to win

But in this loss, again, I will learn to
get up and begin

So I have said my goodbyes with no malice or spite

Because some darkness is bound to find no light

Dairy, my dear friend, I let it all go with such grace

You would be proud of me to know that
I accepted my fate

With all my might, I did my best to put up
a mighty fight

But some nights are endless with no dawn
to break light

I tried my best to be cautious, but I admit
my hope for it all

I know I will find my place one day,
but I still hope you'd call